OUR SOLAR SYSTEM
NEPTUNE
THE WINDIEST PLANET

by Mari Schuh

T0025928

pogo

Ideas for Parents and Teachers

Pogo Books let children practice reading informational text while introducing them to nonfiction features such as headings, labels, sidebars, maps, and diagrams, as well as a table of contents, glossary, and index.

Carefully leveled text with a strong photo match offers early fluent readers the support they need to succeed.

Before Reading

- "Walk" through the book and point out the various nonfiction features. Ask the student what purpose each feature serves.
- Look at the glossary together. Read and discuss the words.

Read the Book

- Have the child read the book independently.
- Invite him or her to list questions that arise from reading.

After Reading

- Discuss the child's questions. Talk about how he or she might find answers to those questions.
- Prompt the child to think more. Ask: Neptune is the farthest planet from the Sun. How does this affect its temperature?

Pogo Books are published by Jump!
5357 Penn Avenue South
Minneapolis, MN 55419
www.jumplibrary.com

Copyright © 2023 Jump!
International copyright reserved in all countries. No part of this book may be reproduced in any form without written permission from the publisher.

Library of Congress Cataloging-in-Publication Data

Names: Schuh, Mari C., 1975- author.
Title: Neptune : the windiest planet / by Mari Schuh.
Description: Minneapolis, MN: Jump!, Inc., [2023]
Series: Our solar system | Includes index.
Audience: Ages 7-10
Identifiers: LCCN 2022031990 (print)
LCCN 2022031991 (ebook)
ISBN 9798885243612 (hardcover)
ISBN 9798885243629 (paperback)
ISBN 9798885243636 (ebook)
Subjects: LCSH: Neptune (Planet)–Juvenile literature.
Classification: LCC QB691 .S38 2023 (print)
LCC QB691 (ebook)
DDC 523.48–dc23/eng20220917
LC record available at https://lccn.loc.gov/2022031990
LC ebook record available at https://lccn.loc.gov/2022031991

Editor: Jenna Gleisner
Designer: Emma Bersie

Photo Credits: Rachel yamagata/Shutterstock, cover (background); SciePro/Shutterstock, cover (Neptune); Tristan3D/Shutterstock, 1; 3DMI/Shutterstock, 3; NASA/JPL, 4, 17; carlosramos1946/Shutterstock, 5 (Neptune); max dallocco/Shutterstock, 5 (Earth); Alex Konon/Shutterstock, 5 (background); sickmoose/Shutterstock, 6-7; NASA images/Shutterstock, 8-9; PixelSquid3d/Shutterstock, 10; ManuMata/Shutterstock, 11; Sergey Fedoskin/Dreamstime, 12-13; NASA/JPL/USGS, 14-15; viktorov.pro/Shutterstock, 16 (Neptune); Stock Store/Shutterstock, 16 (spacecraft); 3quarks/iStock, 18-19; Dima Zel/Shutterstock, 20-21; Nerthuz/Shutterstock, 23.

Printed in the United States of America at Corporate Graphics in North Mankato, Minnesota.

For Bibs

TABLE OF CONTENTS

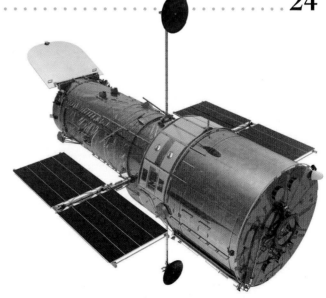

CHAPTER 1

A COLD, WINDY PLANET

The **planet** Neptune is very cold. Strong winds blow. It is the windiest planet in our **solar system**! Neptune has a thick **atmosphere**. It has many clouds and storms.

clouds ·····▶

Neptune is a big planet. It is about four times wider than Earth. If Earth were the size of an apple, Neptune would be the size of a basketball!

We can't see Neptune in the night sky.
Why? It is too far away from Earth.
We need a **telescope** to see Neptune.

TAKE A LOOK!

Neptune is the farthest planet from the Sun. Take a look!

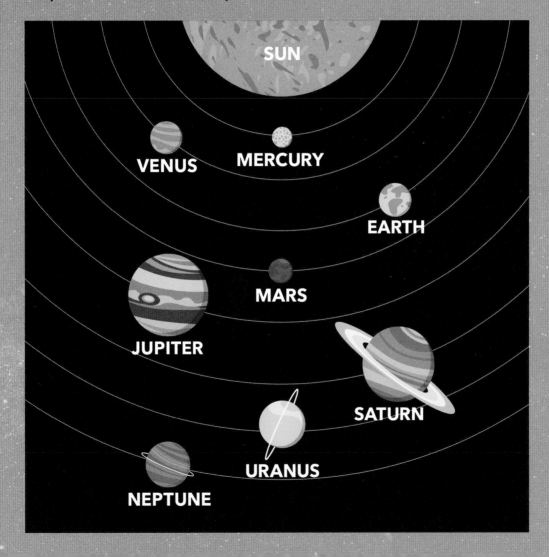

All planets **orbit** the Sun. Because Neptune is the farthest away, the distance it travels is the greatest. It has the longest orbit.

One full orbit around the Sun is one year. One Earth year is 365 days. One Neptune year is 60,190 days!

DID YOU KNOW?

Gravity on Neptune is similar to gravity on Earth. A planet's gravity depends on its size, **mass**, and **density**.

CHAPTER 2

ALL ABOUT NEPTUNE

Because Neptune is far from the Sun, it does not get much sunlight. This makes Neptune very cold. Temperatures are beyond freezing. It can be −373 degrees Fahrenheit (−225 degrees Celsius).

Neptune has five rings. They are made of rocks and dust. They are hard to see.

rings

We can't stand on Neptune. Why not? It does not have a solid surface. Neptune is made mostly of gases. One gas is methane. It gives Neptune its blue color.

TAKE A LOOK!

Neptune's **core** is rocky and icy. That is why it is called an ice giant. What are its other layers? Take a look!

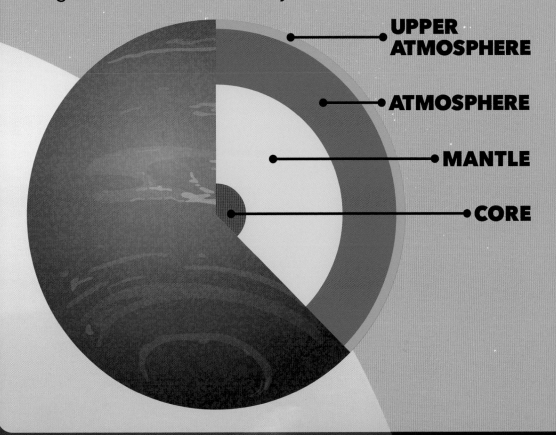

- UPPER ATMOSPHERE
- ATMOSPHERE
- MANTLE
- CORE

Triton

Neptune has 14 moons. The largest is Triton. Triton is almost as big as Earth's Moon.

Triton is very cold. **Geysers** on it spray ice more than five miles (8.0 kilometers) high.

CHAPTER 3

AMAZING DISCOVERIES

Neptune was discovered with a telescope in 1846. *Voyager 2* is the only **spacecraft** that has visited the planet. It flew by the planet in 1989. It discovered some of its moons.

Voyager 2 ⋯⋯▷

Voyager 2 took photos of Neptune's clouds. Higher clouds made shadows on lower clouds. The photos helped scientists measure the distance between the groups of clouds.

Voyager 2 also saw a huge storm on Neptune. The storm was as big as Earth! It was named the Great Dark Spot.

DID YOU KNOW?

Scientists think most storms on Neptune last about two to five years.

Great Dark
Spot

Hubble Space
Telescope

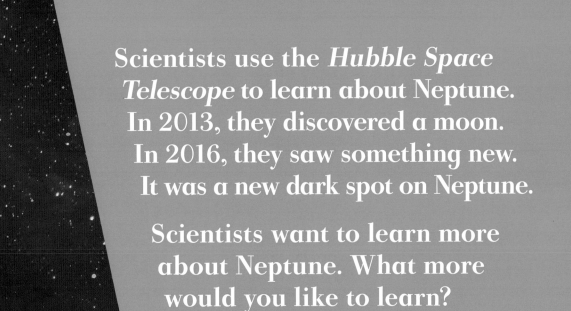

Scientists use the *Hubble Space Telescope* to learn about Neptune. In 2013, they discovered a moon. In 2016, they saw something new. It was a new dark spot on Neptune.

Scientists want to learn more about Neptune. What more would you like to learn?

DID YOU KNOW?

Neptune might have a surprise under its cold clouds. Scientists think a hot ocean might be there!

ACTIVITIES & TOOLS

TRY THIS!

STUDYING WIND SPEED

Neptune has the strongest winds in our solar system. See how fast the wind blows on Earth with this fun activity!

What You Need:

- five small paper cups
- hole punch
- scissors
- tape
- three thin wooden dowels or chopsticks
- empty plastic bottle

1. Use a hole punch to make one hole in the side of four of the paper cups. For the fifth cup, punch four holes just under the cup's rim. The holes should be evenly spaced. This cup will be the center of the device.

2. Slide two of the dowels or chopsticks through the holes in the center cup. They should form an X.

3. Place the other cups on the four ends of the dowels or chopsticks. The cups should be on their sides. They should face the same direction. Use tape to keep them in place.

4. Use the third dowel or chopstick to make a hole in the bottom of the center cup. Push the dowel or chopstick up until it meets the other dowels. Use tape to keep them in place. Then place the center dowel or chopstick into the empty bottle.

5. Set your device outside on a windy day. See how fast the wind blows by how fast the cups spin. The stronger the wind, the faster the cups will spin. Move the device to another area. Do the cups spin slower or faster?

GLOSSARY

atmosphere: The mixture of gases that surrounds a planet.

core: The center, most inner part of a planet.

density: The measure of how heavy or light an object is for its size. Density is measured by dividing an object's mass by its volume.

geysers: Holes in the ground through which ice, water, or steam shoot up into the air.

gravity: The force that pulls things toward the center of a planet and keeps them from floating away.

mass: The amount of physical matter an object has.

orbit: To travel in a circular path around something.

planet: A large body that orbits, or travels in circles around, the Sun.

solar system: The Sun, together with its orbiting bodies, such as the planets, their moons, and asteroids, comets, and meteors.

spacecraft: Vehicles that travel in space.

telescope: A device that uses lenses or mirrors in a long tube to make faraway objects appear bigger and closer.

Triton

INDEX

TO LEARN MORE

Finding more information is as easy as 1, 2, 3.

1. Go to www.factsurfer.com
2. Enter "Neptune" into the search box.
3. Choose your book to see a list of websites.

FACT SURFER